FAITH

First published 2023 by order of the Tate Trustees by Tate Publishing,
a division of Tate Enterprises Ltd, Millbank, London SW1P 4RG
www.tate.org.uk/publishing

A catalogue record for this book is available from the British Library
ISBN 978 1 84976-864 1

Distributed in the United States and Canada by ABRAMS, New York

Library of Congress Control Number applied for

Senior Editor: Alice Chasey
Series Editor: James Finch
Production: Juliette Dupire
Picture Researcher: Roz Hill
Designed by Narrate + Kelly Barrow
Colour reproduction by DL Imaging, London
Printed in Wales by Cambrian Printers

Front cover: Denis Williams, *Moulid el-Nabi* 1959, watercolour, ink, graphite
and paper on paper, 76.2 x 55.5, Tate (detail)

Measurements of artworks are given in centimetres, height before width,
before depth.

FAITH

DEREK OWUSU

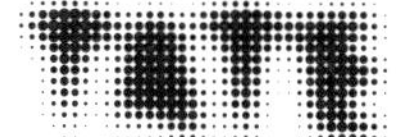

Director's Statement

'Look Again' is a bold new publishing programme from Tate Publishing and Tate Britain. In these books, we are providing a platform for some of the most exciting contemporary voices writing today to explore the national collection of British art in their own way, and reconnect art to our lives today. The books have been developed ahead of the rehang of Tate Britain's collection, which foregrounds many of the artworks discussed here. In this third set of books – *Death* by Sean Burns, *Strangers* by Ismail Einashe *Girlhood* by Claire Marie Healy, and *Faith* by Derek Owusu – we are offered unique perspectives on a wide range of artworks across British history, and encouraged to look closely, and to look again.

Alex Farquharson, Director, Tate Britain

In *Leaving the Atocha Station* (2011), the debut novel by Ben Lerner, there is a description of a man bursting into tears in front of Rogier van der Weyden's *The Descent from the Cross* c.1435. Lerner's protagonist wonders if the man is having what he himself feels incapable of experiencing – a profound experience of art – and goes on to express his intense suspicion of those who claim to have encountered such a feeling. Reading this passage, I recall my head's slight gesture in agreement. But it was a retrospective accord, a reach for feelings and thoughts that had left me by that point but which I could still conjure and instinctively apply to the character's insight.

Visiting galleries is not something I have ever thought of or planned to do. There was something churchlike about them, entering them a duty that spoke of moral character, which made me uncomfortable and sometimes rebellious. I don't say that with pride; it's just the way things were. I've never slipped into bed with the rising excitement that the next day I would be standing in front of a piece of art where an exchange would take place, arms behind my back, tender skin of one hand resting in the other's rough palm, a look of fulfilment slowly filling my face, nourishing tides almost spilling when I tilted my head to better see what the artist hoped to convey. Nope: whenever I found myself in a gallery, it was either impromptu, part of a ruse after a meal to attach some culture to the impression of my personality, or because I was waiting for someone, you know, trying to kill time, and the gallery was shelter from the cold. Though often it was as if the cold followed me. No painting or sculpture, no matter how long I looked, aroused any revelation or warmth. I assumed that everyone around me at the time was acting, taking part in a collective melodrama that of course I had forgotten to read the script for. Because I could not imitate it without feeling uncomfortable – the act of looking and seeming to appreciate the art appeared more impressive to me than the art itself.

Standing and looking at art. It is ironic that the painting that began to shift my perspective of 'profound experiences of art' is one in which a man, we assume, can be interpreted in a similar posture: *Wanderer above the Sea of Fog* 1818 by Caspar David Friedrich. It hung above a friend's single bed, for the same reason, I assumed, people went to art galleries. One day, I got as close to it as possible without climbing onto his mattress. My shins pressed into the bedframe. I stared at the image, trying to get it – and then I felt myself relax, instinctively knowing something about this wanderer, believing in what he was feeling as he stared, in turn, into the abyss and rocky landscape, fog engulfing the horizon. Standing at that peak, I could 'intuit' that he was looking for something – something, I knew, I was yet to find. This wanderer, I sensed, though he was lost, was content to be so: he had no compulsion to take leave of those cliffs, to leap from his precipice. In time, he would navigate the grey, but for now he would look and wait to be able to embrace the world. Fleetingly, I felt what I now think of as faith: faith that he, I, we, would find the way. I want to feel such assurance again.

Faith. If we all ceased to believe, would the thread be cut, planes plummet from the sky? Would technology stop, would one foot fail to follow another, would a rapture take us into the air? Faith, to me, is believing what you don't understand and can't comprehend, resolute in your ignorance, because you trust in humanity – in the stories we've woven and the narratives we've constructed and go on building each day; in other people; in something beyond you, your understanding. You choose to believe that outside of your experience and your line of sight, things are carrying on to keep everything in motion, on an inevitable, structured path. We recognise and react to it, retrospectively or with foresight, through visions or assurances from those we trust, believe in. Humanity is a story of faith. As crude as my example may be, we live in a world of belief and of faith. And though it's almost instinctive to see where faith has been, will be and is, still we must be taught, often by example.

Sometimes it's the shy and minuscule that can lead us on our way. Material that has no desire to be seen can touch us, dilating the world so we can attempt to walk through its centre.

I was raised in a religious house. I was forced to go to church every Sunday, read the Bible with my mother every evening and let her pray for me and anoint my head whenever she felt it necessary. This performance, the performance of piety, I knew well and could easily participate in. My mother was a virtuoso, so adept that I came to realise it was not an act at all. Like the man in Lerner's novel bursting into tears before *The Descent from the Cross*, my mother, with every energetic prayer, burst into tears before the silver crucified Jesus hanging from our wall. The design was crude, the silver paint over the plastic figure peeling and the gold crown of thorns turning a shade of orange. But all that meant nothing. What my mother was looking at was not what she saw. She was seeing her entire life, choices and decisions, flights and landings, every unlit path taken conspiring to ensure her arrival. It was the representation of faith that to her was so lachrymose and moving. It was faith, beyond the image, touching everything in her life, and what was objectively in front of her did not matter.

I saw my mother look at me in this same way, a long unbroken stare until I asked her 'What?' and she'd tell me she could see the glory of God in my face. Special occasions, she would weep into her wrapping paper, sometimes leaving gifts visible through their soggy encasing, or into her ntoma as she ironed it on our floor, preparing for a wedding or a funeral, each of which seemed to carry the same emotional weight. To my surprise, she even tested the waterproof finish on my first hardback. Wherever they rested, her eyes carried with them paths to or recognition of faith. They were observing a diversion, one already traversed, or its possibility, ways to infinite emotion and thought that would always lead back to the source: humanity, its creations and, beyond, the realisation of boundless existence.

The mistake I made when I watched my mother as a child or as I watched those in galleries as an adult was assuming that because I could not experience it, or had only glimpsed it once, then they could not either. But now that I've matured in many ways, and with my mother being the closest person to me, I want to see the world through her eyes, ricocheting off the light of faith and creating an experience that will appear real to whoever decides to observe me – or rather, to read me. This book is that opportunity. And maybe I'll come out of this seeing more than I have been.

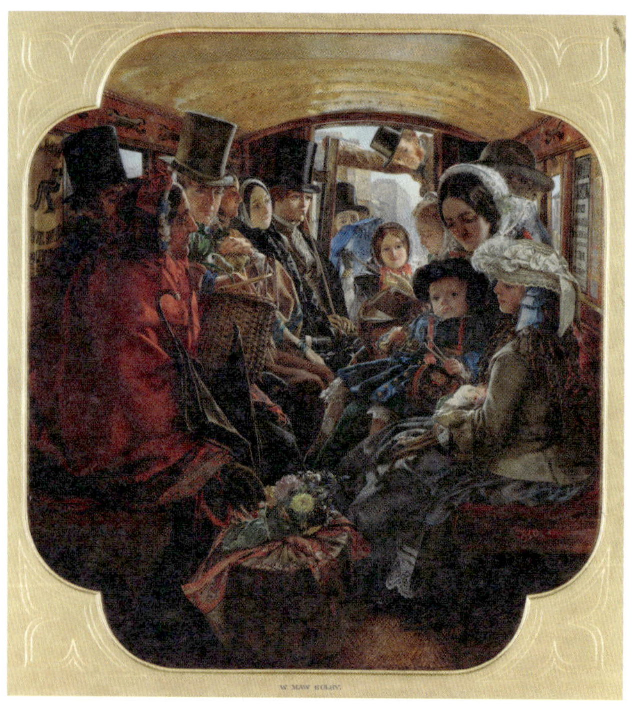

William Maw Egley, *Omnibus Life in London* 1859, oil paint on canvas, 44.8 x 41.9, Tate

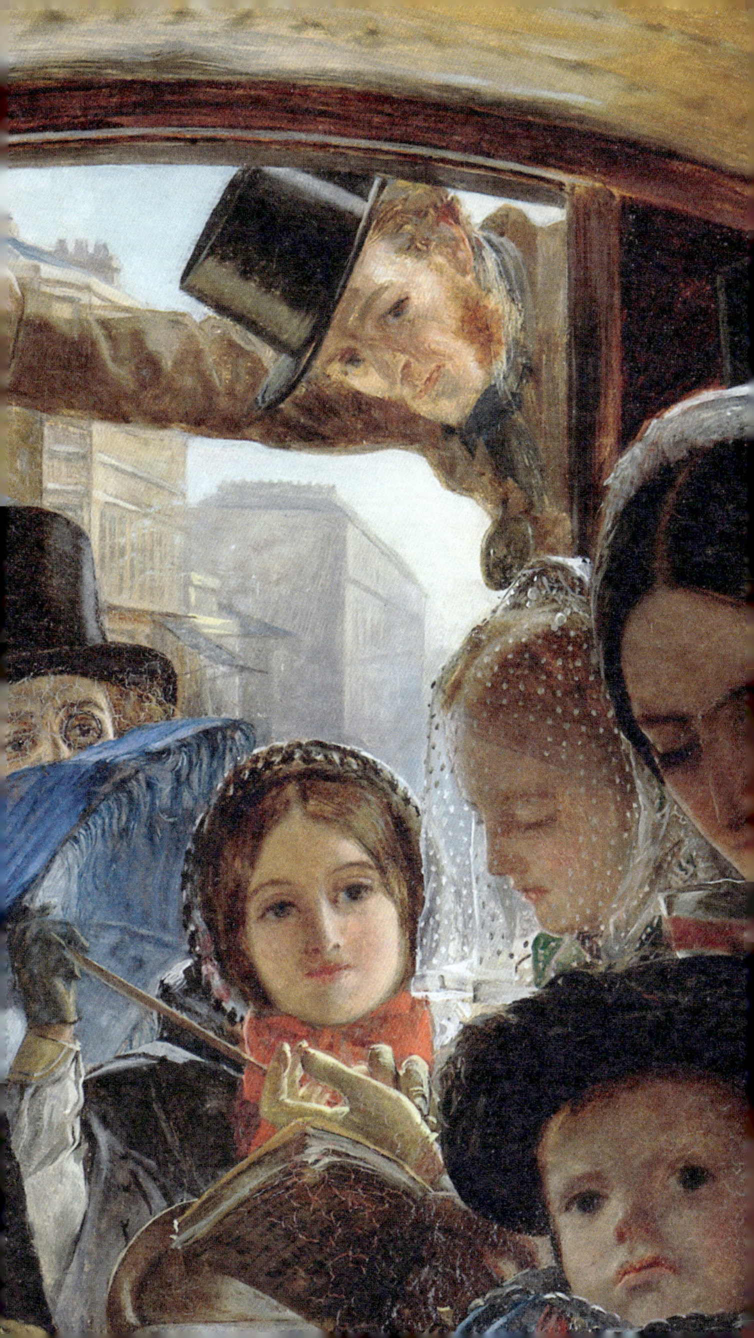

"THE TRO TRO MOVES ON, EVERYONE SURE
THEY WILL ARRIVE AT THEIR DESTINATION,
SHOULD THEY PAY THE TOLL, SHOULD THEY
EVEN FALL."

Sweat clings to bodies, a drop exacts another toll, all resisting contact with the slow and lithe, sticking and weaving, malleable limbs working their way through and over the seated, who, when the tro tro dips in potholes, lifting each of them from their place, remain still aside from adjusting their bottoms to try and find the exact feeling of comfort that was just disrupted. The boy collecting money has no seat, seems to float between two distant headrests or above the bodies who must eventually raise their hands to him in offering. Another pothole and a little girl with two divided puffs of hair is raised as though an invisible string in her parting had been tugged by the boy above, then begins to fall away from her mother's lap. Mother and daughter stretch out arms and the sound of hand on wrist like a solitary clap of exhausted palms. The girl is pulled back to her mother's knee, no one turns or worries what could be. The tro tro moves on, everyone sure they will arrive at their destination, should they pay the toll, should they even fall. The little girl looks around, ready to find the boy from above, a few coins singing off each other in her hand, and her mother looking away, seeming to pay no mind but with a tighter hold around the waist of her child.

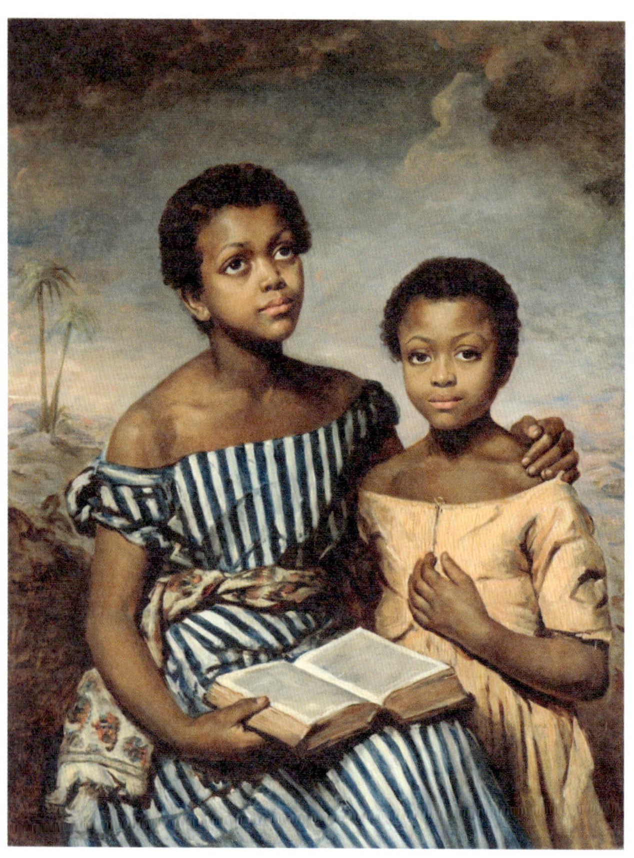

Emma Soyer, *Two Children with a Book* 1831, oil paint on canvas,
91.7 x 71.6, Tate

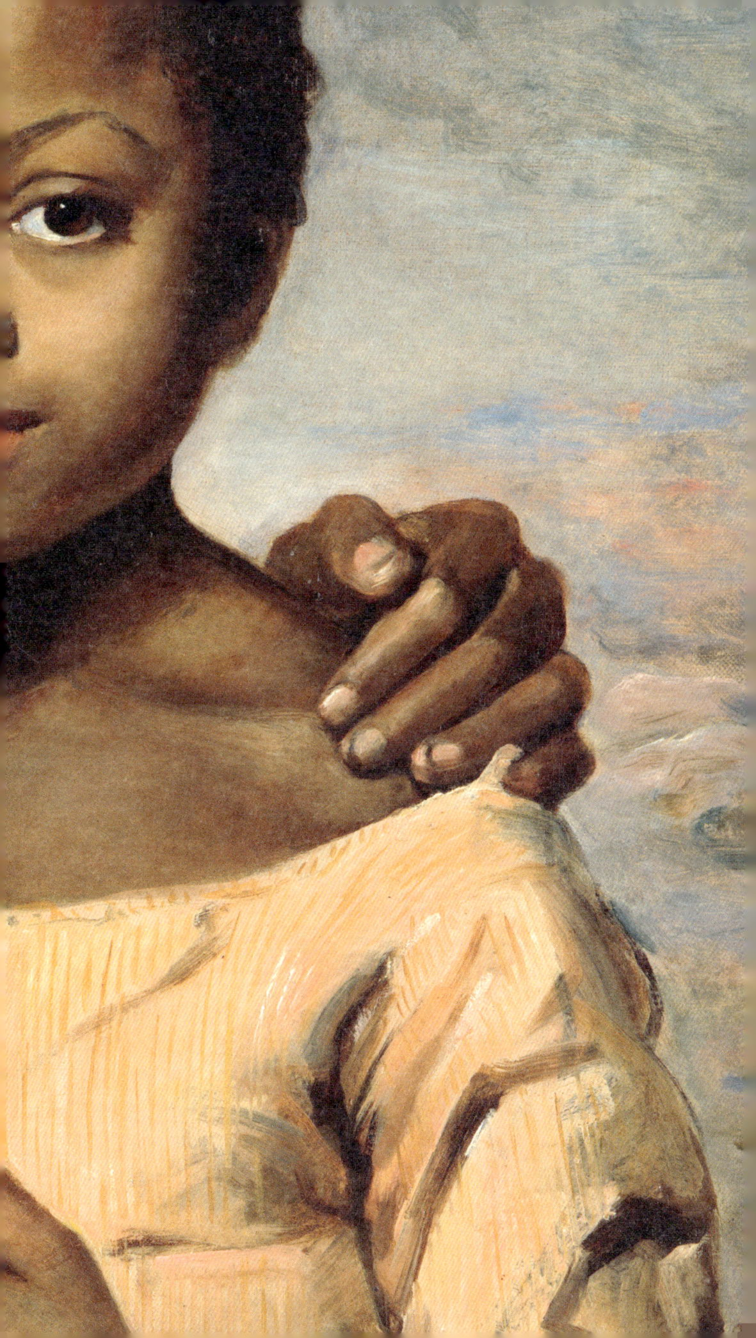

Thousands of gifts were to be handed over, wrapped, protected, contained within paper and leather. And those gifts, as they were or connected to others, imparted their own alms. Before she left for the UK her mother handed her an English Bible. Each word was like a tiny deity, odious, waiting for her to open her mouth and attempt to pronounce, then they'd pounce, choking her with her own accent. If she looked for too long at the markings, she'd become dizzy, closing the book with all the zeal of her weakening arms, the Bible between her palms like a barrier to a clap of praise. But her mother would lean over from when she sat on the floor crushing her pestle into the mortar, and open it up again, and say, in Twi, 'Please, for me, try again?' Days with scattered words pass her till she can peer through and see her family waving goodbye, and as the craft tilted to the sky, she remembered her mother placing the book in her lap, spread on a page that then begins every reading. And today, a finger through that page and another, my mum dances around her living room, crooning and clapping, one palm against the leather cover of the gift her mother gave her.

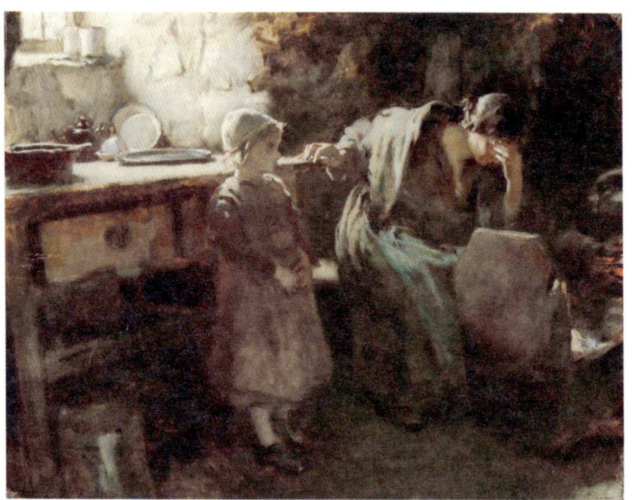

Frank Holl, *Hushed* 1877, oil paint on canvas, 67 x 77, Tate

"WITH HER FACE TOWARDS HER WINDOW, SHE CLOSES HER EYES AND THE SUN PROVIDES A MOLTEN ORANGE, OBSCURED FOR A SECOND AS A SHADOW PASSES."

The sound and sight of cockcrow evokes a day the world could come to its end, but with no one to rise because already the kitchen is full with porous souls, tears indistinguishable from salty rivulets emerging and falling on the pale skin that no one thought could see such colour. The mother watches her child's breathing to slow her own, to calm or ensure they go together. If a sickness takes one it takes all. Around them the sound of feet through the dust, potholes filled then emptied, the sudden awareness of many at roost, shouts as a neighbour lifts her palm frond to shoo away the reptilian. The mother, child in her lap, keeps her eyes away, concealed from a face that asks for so little, something so worthless it now seems, and yet still her mother cannot pass it on her own. With her face towards her window, she closes her eyes and the sun provides a molten orange, obscured for a second as a shadow passes.

'Hello, ma.' She opens up and turns: there, a man in white crouching to enter her home. His sleeves rolled up, brown at their ruffled ends matching the interior where the top button's undone with a tie hanging loose. 'Ma, hello. Can I enter? Is this the one who is sick?'

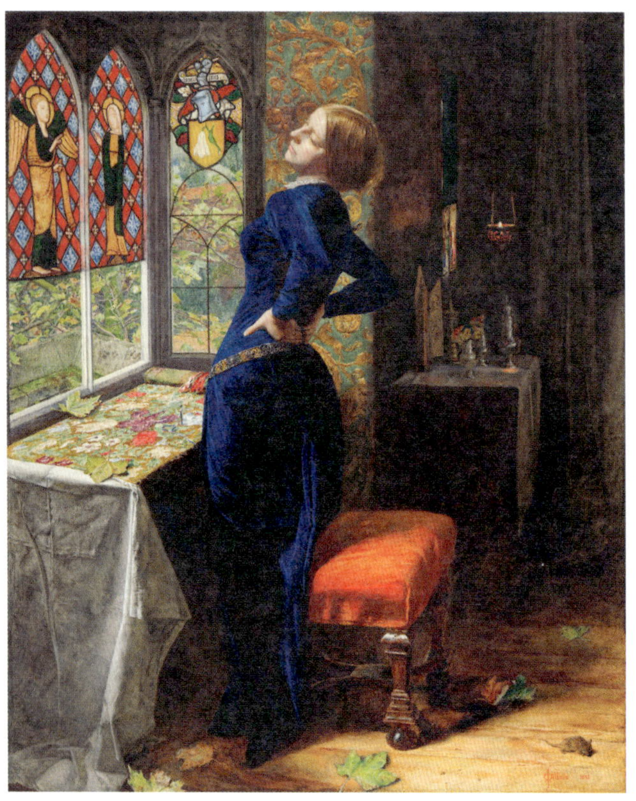

John Everett Millais, *Mariana* 1851, oil paint on wood, 59.7 x 49.5, Tate

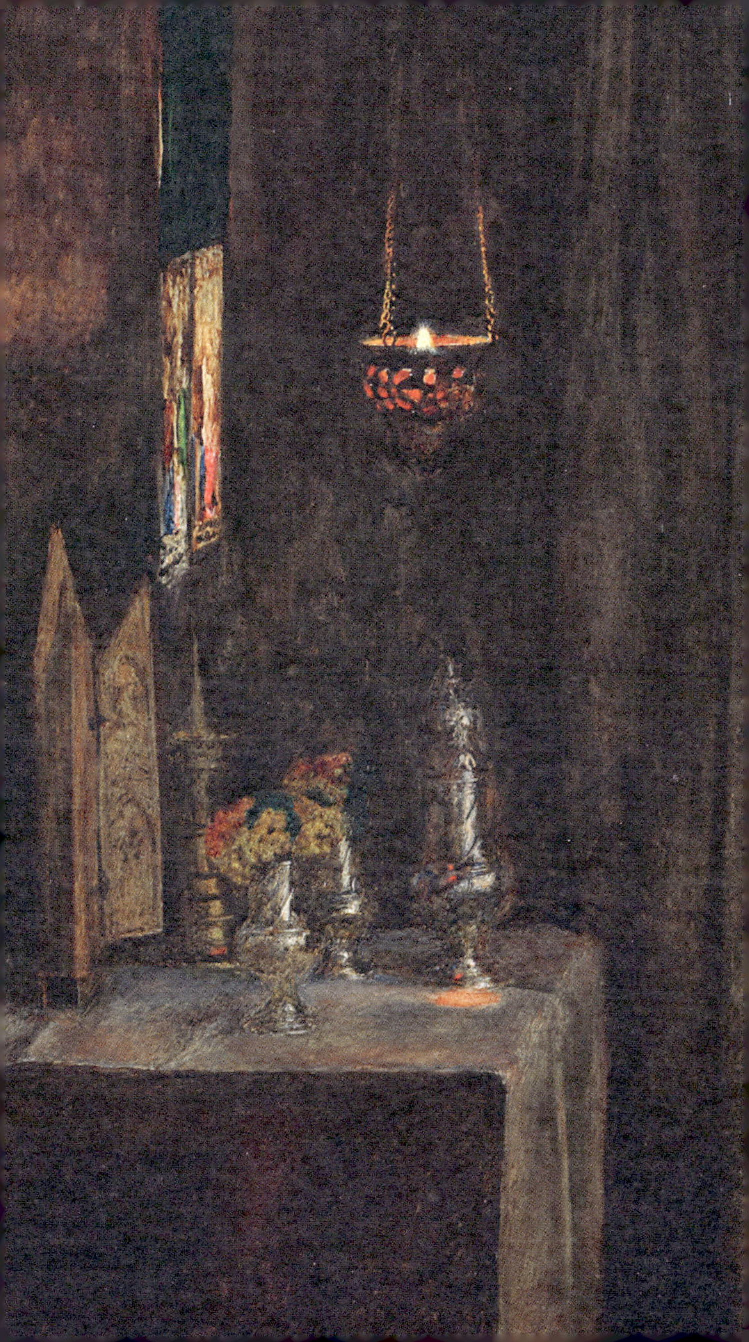

A chill so full and ubiquitous pieces could be held and hidden from all those that will follow on its breeze, a piece of weather cut off from climbing and touching the spine of a working woman unused to a climate that seems to desire to keep you out rather than embrace you like the touch of humidity of back home, so warm it draws tears from the skin. Vulnerable air, unlike the sharp harshness that seeps through the closed windows and beneath doors, overcoming the piled cloth that attempts to dissuade its entry, an entreaty is the sound of cracking joints that take their time to submit to the aches of autumn. A mother adds layer after layer until bulk may hold its ground when she steps out, avoiding the fallen leaves, scared of the sound of something so soft being crushed underfoot, but she lapses, clenching her teeth to disguise the sounds or suppress the thought of brittle being ripped apart. She carries on but looks back, seeing the crumbled outer body of the leaf, but at the centre, it remains green, soft but unbroken, veins still visible, seeming to pulse with the confidence that what has been torn from its body will only give way to a new shape.

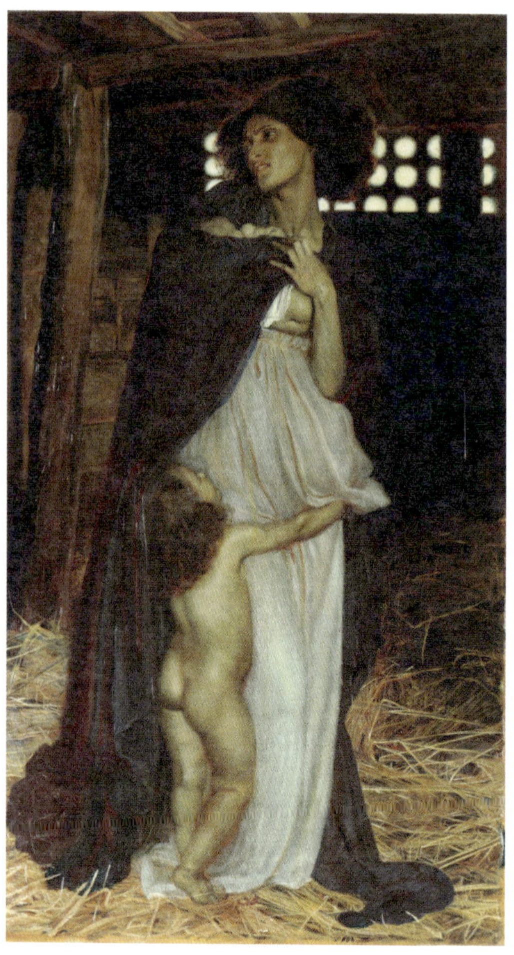

William Blake Richmond, *The Slave* c.1865, oil paint on canvas,
91.4 x 52.7, Tate

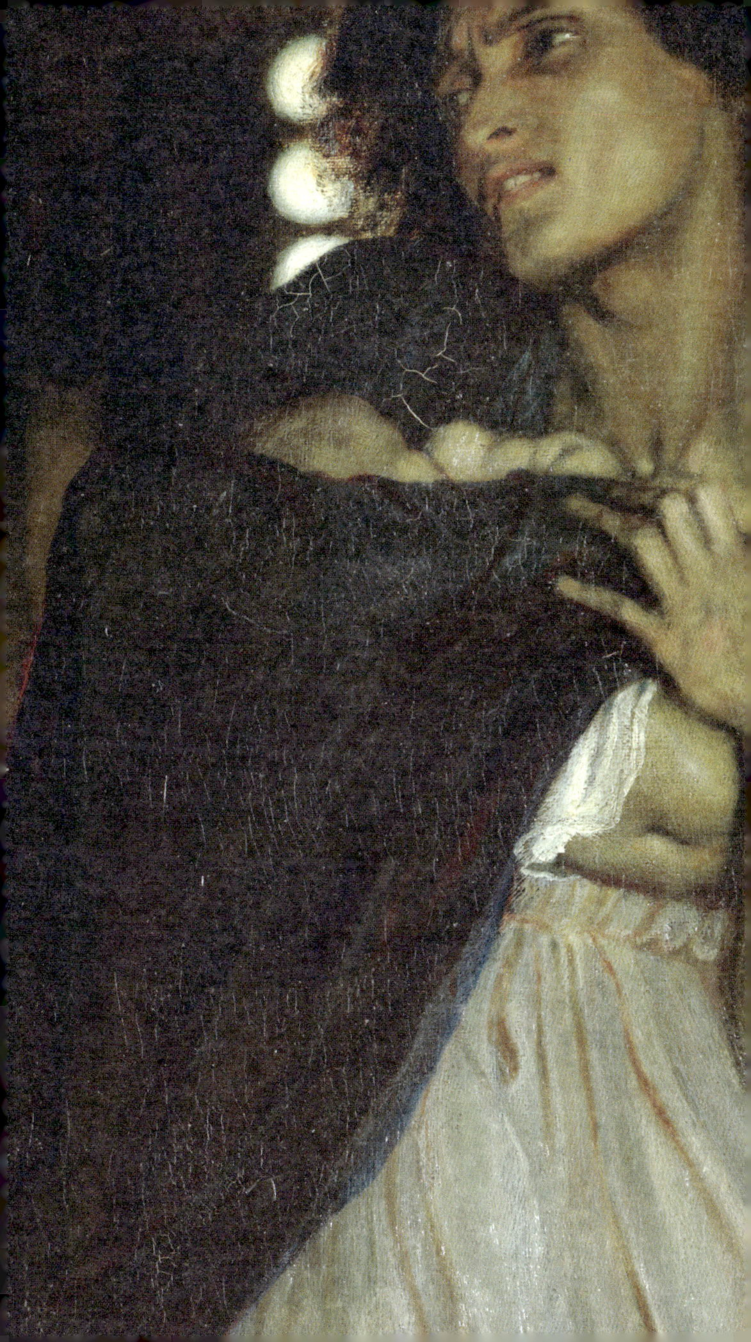

Experience relayed as story then pieced together
to become a memory of the first telling after
its restoration.

Ma, around the outside of the clay house, slides, heavy, weighted feet sweeping the floor, the sand and stony ground only painful on her sole today, when the sting pardons the pain trying to touch every part of her, in the darkness each contraction seen like a splintering bolt flashing throughout her body. She bends over, clenched fists on her knees and lets her chest rumble with a suppressed cry, feels as though there's another layer on her breast, smooth, that a finger could go through, Yesu, she stands and walks again. She could, should run, but where would she land, finish, as the son beats her and Awurade watches on as salt clings to her face. Wet feet follow her, her sisters, anointed, who stepped into the warm water that fell from this sibling's suffering, who has been through this before, but not like this. Their fear is kept wrapped up, they catch something spill each time they adjust their wrapper under their chest. Ma, she carries on, pausing, asking what is the meaning, her sisters tell her not to speak, circling and warming the centre of her back, looking around for the man one of the children was sent to collect. Ma, stands straight, looks up, to be engulfed, to know the pitch of the sky, closing her eyes hoping for what it imitates to become actual, and from beneath her a body begins to fall.

This telling says the baby put both its hands on
Ma's leg, a stance taking issue with the world,
and pushed upward, so distraught, not ready to
be brought forth in such a way, no hands to be
laid beneath it, or under it, the only thing that
could catch it is the dusk, sand, dirt and clay. But
this refusal was eased when the sisters ran between
Ma's knees and six hands laid the ground for rebirth,
each one humming a gospel that in the humidity felt
as though the melody could cool the earth, sounds
sending a chill stopping the devil's play, bonsam,
hey! All will be fine – the words in this strain, God
spoke through them and said this world too is mine.

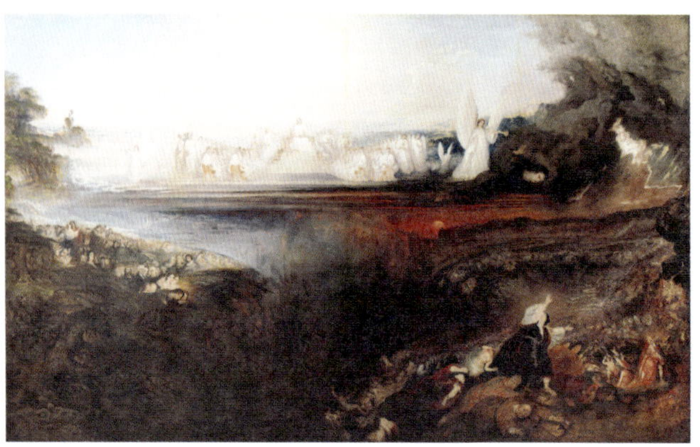

John Martin, *The Last Judgement* 1853, oil paint on canvas,
240 x 368.5, Tate

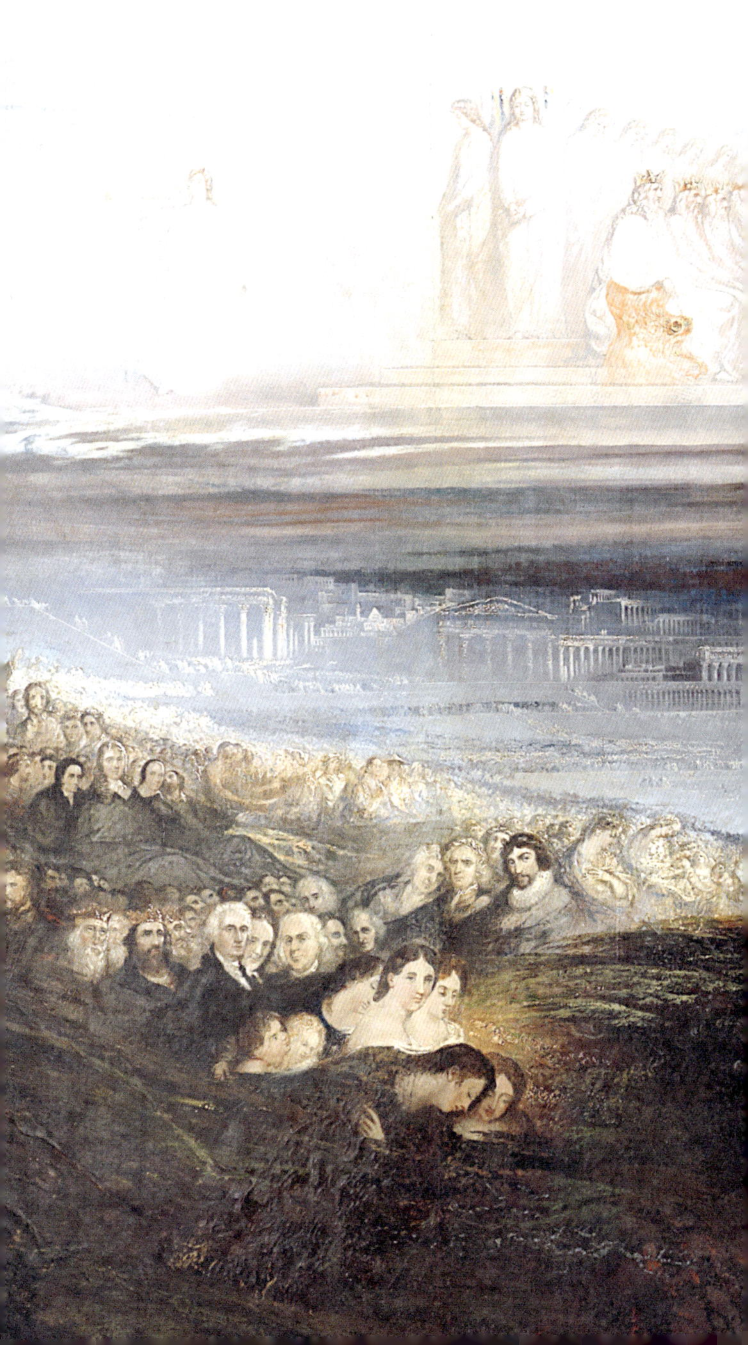

Their hem strokes the sky. She leans in to see two wings separate and a pinion splitting the blue until she can see through and witness what is before her and after. A light thrown towards passes through her and splinters as the prism of her life takes shape in the distance, coming together to be witnessed and razed, solid and broken. Then the last touch of land on her toes; her last moment in its throes. Her arms fall to her sides, as a trumpet undulates the sky.

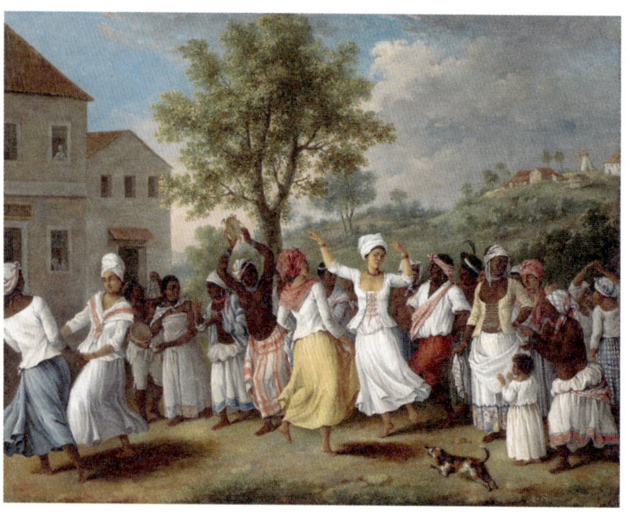

Agostino Brunias, *Dancing Scene in the Caribbean*, 1764-96, oil paint on canvas, 50.8 x 66, Tate

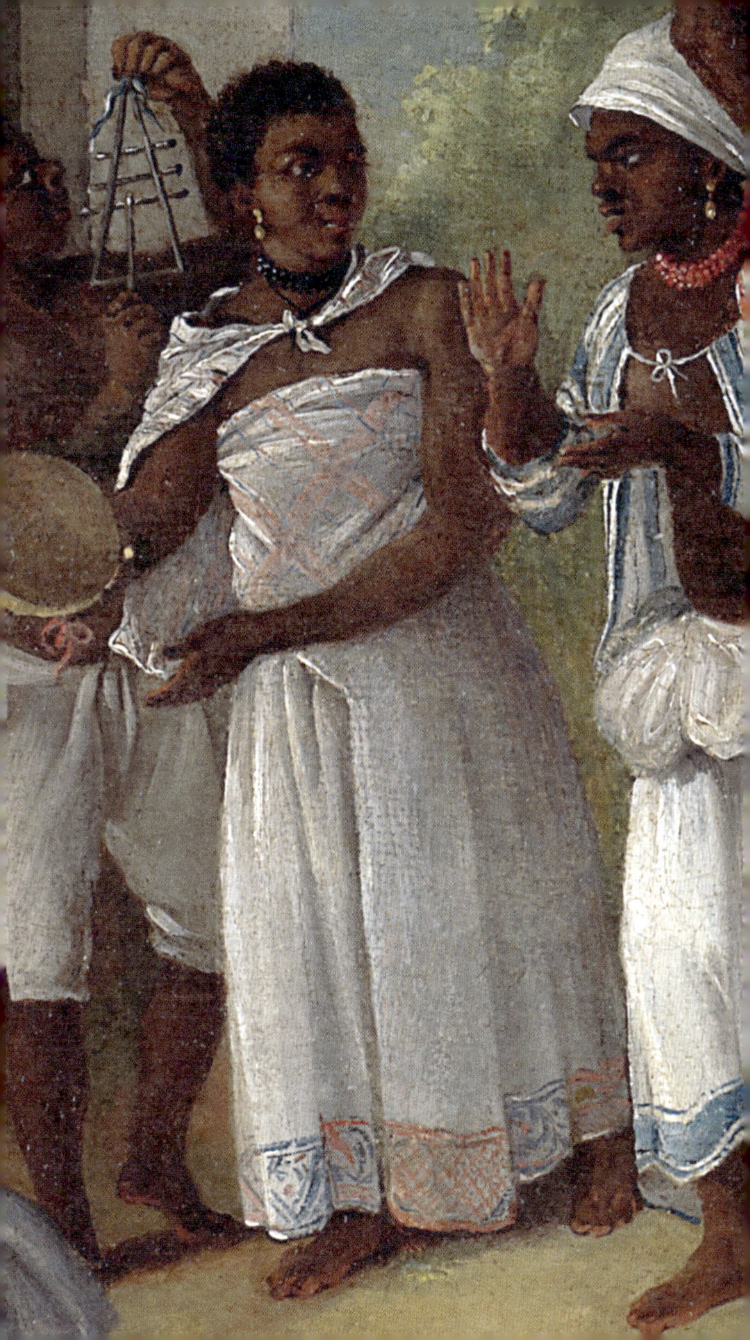

"THE CROONS OPEN WOUNDS IN THE BLUE,
SLIDING THROUGH TO FIND THE OTHER VOICES
SAYING GOODBYE, TOGETHER EVENTUALLY THE
CACOPHONY BURIES THE SKY"

A step closer to each other and a step away, the white handkerchiefs in the air a bleached blaze, a cool ember in each hand flickering, its tail touching and blessing the celebrated explorer, then raised again to join the flare in fighting back the passing days, each way you look another shuffle, in the rain, upon dried clay, mothers, aunts, sisters and mamas giving their daughters away. The croons open wounds in the blue, sliding through to find the other voices saying goodbye, together eventually the cacophony buries the sky, the entirety of Western land understands this dropless cry. A passage to relieve them of their region, only Westerners are blind to their steps, though still they dance as their worlds intersect, at a distance, miles like the walks to the varying villages fled. Their rejoicing can still summon a squall, lives on the wind, an open window to let ancestors and kin folk in, a gust beneath a handkerchief lifts fire once again, knowing there are still many journeys yet to begin.

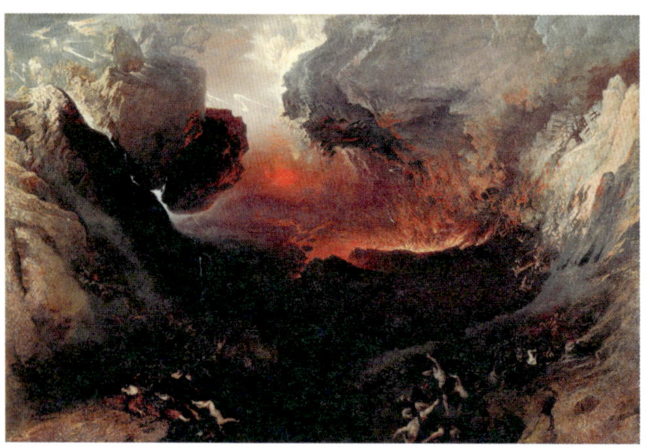

John Martin, *The Great Day of His Wrath* 1851–3, oil paint on canvas, 240 x 347, Tate

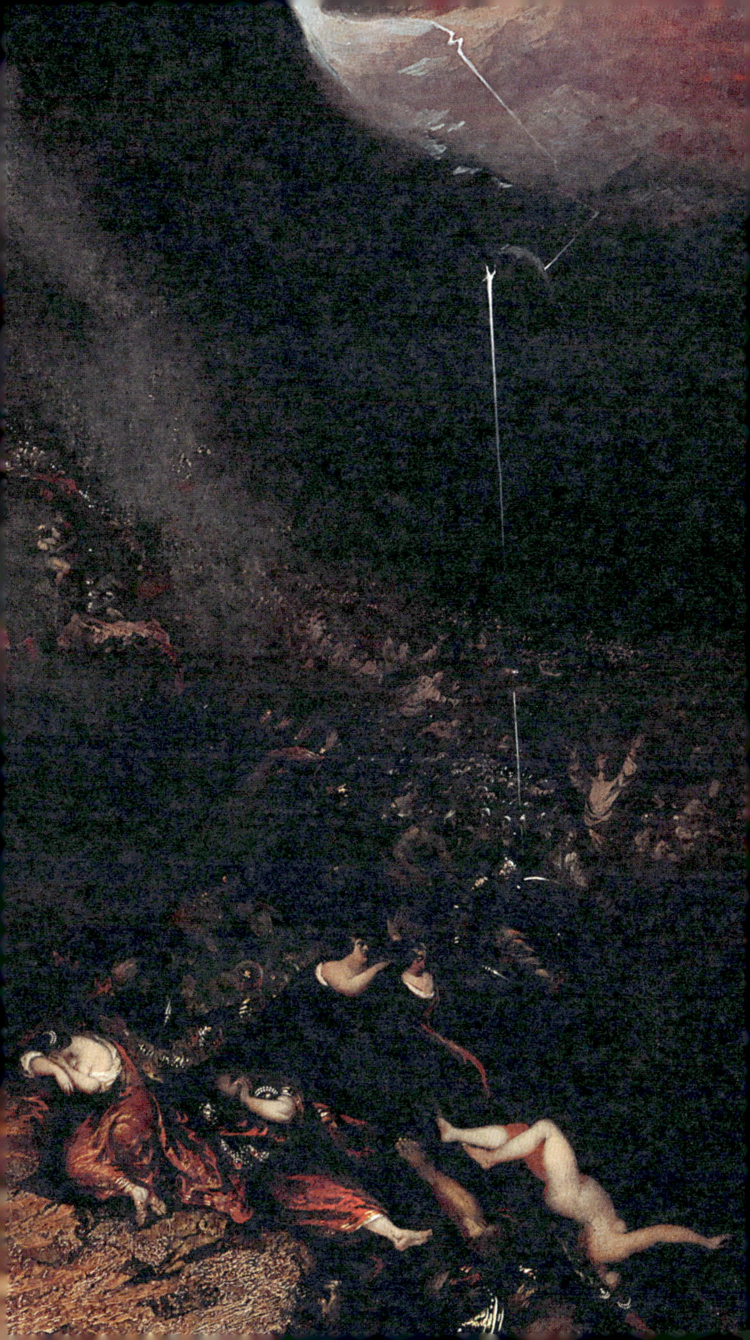

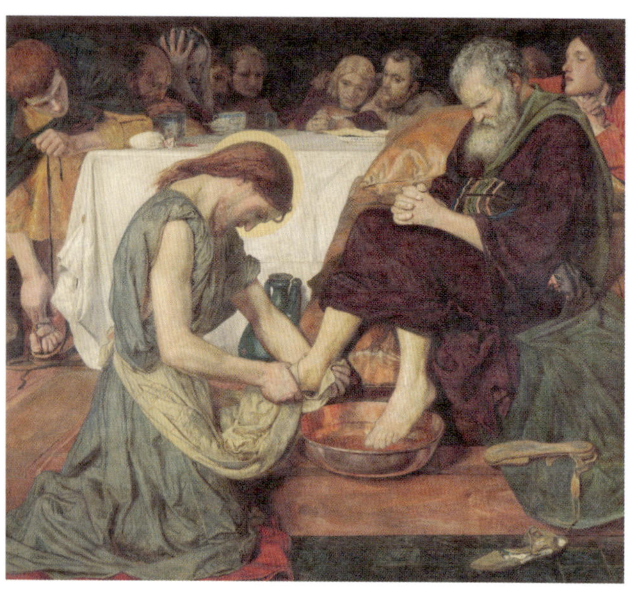

Ford Madox Brown, *Jesus Washing Peter's Feet* 1852–6, oil paint on canvas, 116.8 x 133.3, Tate

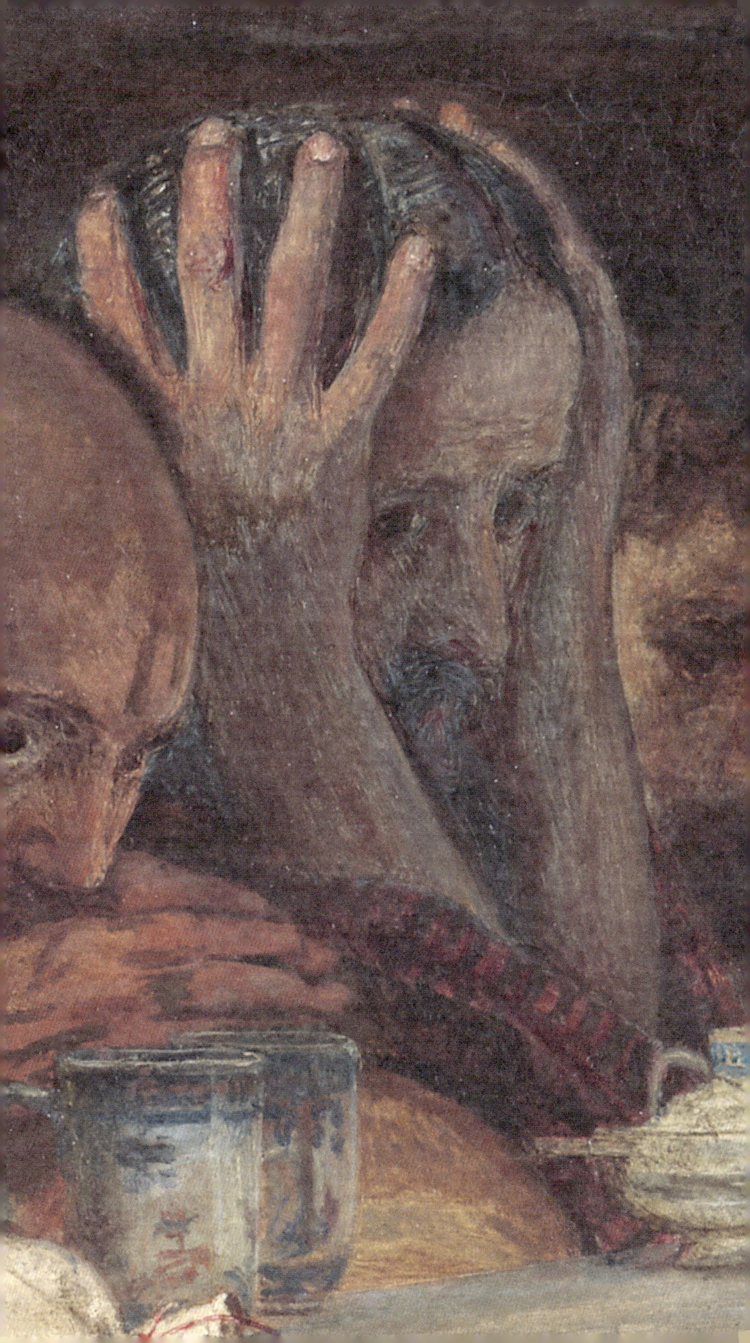